T

Rising from the ~~~~~~~~~~~~ ~~ oppression and
banishment to the religious underground, Neo-Paganism
is now emerging as a viable body of transformative spirituality. Rather than providing dogmatic answers, Neo-
Paganism focuses on offering powerful techniques, such
as ritual and meditation, through which you can search
for your own answers.

What are the fundamental beliefs that unite the
many different paths of this diverse religion?

- Everything is connected to everything else
- Everything is cyclic
- Nature knows best: the Earth is a living deity and
  animals are no less important than humans
- Deity exists in everything
- Paganism is polytheistic, with special honor to the
  Goddess
- Ethics: "If it harm none, do what you will"
- Personal empowerment
- Honoring the elements and their correspondence
  with aspects of our experience
- Neo-Pagans are non-hierarchical
- The Circle as a ritual formation
- Neo-Pagans have a positive attitude about their
  bodies and sexuality
- Worship in conjunction with the cycles of the Moon
  and the Sun

Learn more about the magic of Neo-Paganism—an old
religion for a new age!

About the Author

Anodea Judith serves as Priestess and former president of the Church of All Worlds, helping to run its subsidiary organizations, Forever Forests, Nemeton, Ecosophical Research Association, and the Holy Order of Mother Earth (H.O.M.E.). She is the founder and director of LIFEWAYS, a school for the study of consciousness and healing arts, located in Northern California and is the author of a well-known book on the chakras, *Wheels of Life*. Anodea has studied acupressure, yoga, bioenergetics, psychic healing and reading, gestalt therapy, radical psychiatry, ritual magic, and shamanism. Her workshops have been offered coast to coast, and her writings have appeared in a variety of publications.

To Write to the Author

If you wish to contact the author or would like more information about this book, please write to the author in care of Llewellyn Worldwide and we will forward your request. Both the author and publisher appreciate hearing from you and learning of your enjoyment of this book and how it has helped you. Llewellyn Worldwide cannot guarantee that every letter written to the author can be answered, but all will be forwarded. Please write to:

Anodea Judith
c/o Llewellyn Worldwide
P.O. Box 64383-567, St. Paul, MN 55164-0383, U.S.A.

Please enclose a self-addressed, stamped envelope for reply,
or $1.00 to cover costs.
If outside U.S.A., enclose international postal reply coupon.

Free Catalog from Llewellyn

For more than 90 years Llewellyn has brought its readers knowledge in the fields of metaphysics and human potential. Learn about the newest books in spiritual guidance, natural healing, astrology, occult philosophy, and more. Enjoy book reviews, new age articles, a calendar of events, plus current advertised products and services. To get your free copy of *Llewellyn's New Worlds of Mind and Spirit*, send your name and address to:

Llewellyn's New Worlds of Mind and Spirit
P.O. Box 64383-567, St. Paul, MN 55164-0383, U.S.A.

LLEWELLYN'S VANGUARD SERIES

The Truth About

NEO-PAGANISM

by Anodea Judith

Author of
Wheels of Life

1994
Llewellyn Publications
P.O. Box 64383, St. Paul, MN 55164-0383
U.S.A.

For permissions, or for serialization, condensation, or for adaptations, write the Publisher.

First Edition
First Printing, 1994

International Standard Book Number:
1–56718–567–3

LLEWELLYN PUBLICATIONS
A Division of Llewellyn Worldwide, Ltd.
P.O. Box 64383, St. Paul, MN 55164-0383

Other Books by Anodea Judith

Wheels of Life

The Truth About Chakras

The Sevenfold Journey (Crossing Press)

THE TRUTH ABOUT NEO-PAGANISM

Neo-Paganism is the fastest growing religion in America today. Feminism, environmental crises, a need for a practical spirituality, and rising disillusionment with hierarchical world religions are bringing people of all ages back to the religions of their ancestors. Rising from the ashes of 5,000 years of oppression and banishment to the religious underground, Neo-Paganism is now emerging as a viable body of transformative spirituality. Those who discover it are finding a religion that honors women and nature, without denigrating men, a philosophy that empowers the individual, a framework that addresses our troubled world, and a religious experience abundant with creativity and joy. Rather than providing dogmatic answers, Neo-Paganism focuses on asking relevant questions and offering powerful techniques, such as ritual and meditation, through which people can search for their own answers. A religion of personal and planetary empowerment, Neo-Paganism is rising to the forefront of spiritual culture.

Accurate estimates of the current Pagan population are difficult to ascertain. Because of past oppression, (see **History**, below) which still causes some people to lose their jobs or children, or to be the targets of harassment, many Pagans fear speaking out publicly about their religion. Yet there are 500 Pagan periodicals published nationwide, each with a readership from 50 to 30,000, and the numbers are growing rapidly. Margot Adler, in her updated social study of the Neo-Pagan movement, *Drawing Down the Moon*, estimates the population to be around 50,000–100,000 *active* self-proclaimed Neo-Pagans. Her latest version is dated 1986, and at the current growth rates in periodical subscriptions and memberships in Pagan organizations, the number may be three to five times that high by the time of this writing in 1992.

My personal estimate is that there are at least one million people in the United States who would claim Paganism as their religion of choice, were it to be included in the national census. These may include practitioners of many different traditions, including Native Americans, ceremonial magicians, Witches, Druids, feminist theologians who honor the Goddess, Hindus, some Buddhists, and those who follow shamanic paths. Still others would call themselves Pagan if they had informed knowledge of what the term really means. Many people who receive an explanation of Pagan beliefs say, "That's what I've always believed, but I never knew what to call it!" They do not change their beliefs to join the movement, but instead find a movement that is in harmony with the values and beliefs that they already hold.

What is this movement, what is it based upon, and what effect might it have on the cultural and spiritual framework of the Western world? What are its beliefs and what does it offer its practitioners?

From the Latin word *paganus*, meaning "country dweller," the term Neo-Paganism describes *a modern social and religious movement based on the reconstruction and adaptation of our ancestral polytheistic nature religions.* The prefix "neo" is used to distinguish modern Pagan practice from those of the ancestors, because many of the rites have changed and evolved along with our culture. Believing that there is no real separation between self and environment, between races or sexes, Neo-Pagans see their world as an incredibly rich and complex interconnected web of which all things are a part. This view of interconnectedness empowers the individual as an agent of change. As part of the web, we are able to effect subtle changes within it—changes that help to bring it back into balance once again, from its precarious state of environmental threat, social oppression, and spiritual bankruptcy.

Neo-Paganism is a religion connecting the worlds of myth and reality, heaven and earth, life and death, person and planet. It is a religion that is inclusive rather than exclusive, life-affirming rather than self-denying, cyclic rather than linear. Predating Christianity by more than 30,000 years, it is the common ancestral religion of our people and our planet, once brutally repressed, and now returning at a time of great crisis and need.

This little booklet will give you an idea of the history, the basic beliefs and practices, and the many threads and styles that make up this colorful tapestry that is at once religion and social movement. Neo-Paganism is complex and varied, without rigorous dogma. It is held together more by experience than belief, love rather than fear. It is an exciting journey of reconnection between humans and the gods, bridging the gulf of alienation that so plagues our world.

HISTORY

Long ago, when humans lived in closer proximity to Nature, we experienced ourselves as enfolded into an intricate and wonderful web. All around us, as far as we could see, were the trees and the grasses, the flowers and the mountains, the Sun and the Moon and the stars. Our effect upon the environment that surrounded us was minimal. Its effect upon us, however, was not. We were dependent upon the growing season's benevolence to keep us fed and alive through a winter we hoped would not be too harsh or too long. We were dependent on the abundance of game for our food, the blessings of fate on our children and our tribe, the gentle presence of rain without the ferocity of dangerous storms.

This web around us had power beyond our understanding. It was alive, as we were, yet so much larger and more profound. As women in our tribe swelled in the belly and gave birth, so did the world around us: the animals gave birth in the spring, the trees and plants put forth their fruit. The miracle of human life through the bodies of women was equated with the miracle of the life-giving properties of the earth we lived on, and was seen as divine.

This intricate environmental web was a deity to be worshiped and honored. Because it brought forth food in the way that women brought forth life, the divine was worshiped as feminine. Today, we think of her as Mother Earth or Mother Nature, for she was the universal mother of us all. We do not know the ancient words for her, but numerous figurines of women with pregnant bellies and pendulous breasts were found throughout Old Europe, dating back as far as 30,000 years (see figures 1, 2, and 3.) From 3,000 sites of the Neolithic and Chalcolithic era in southeastern Europe, some 30,000 sculptures of clay, marble, bone, copper, or gold have been found,[1] all attesting to an apparent reverence for life and an honoring of the feminine as a fundamental aspect of ancient religion, focused on the Earth Mother.

While ancient tribes honored a Goddess as prime deity, the Earth Mother was not alone. In hunting societies, the men would dress in the skins and horns of the animals, in hopes to better the hunt by calling the game to themselves, as evidenced by ancient cave paintings. As medicine man, the tribal chief was also imbued with magical

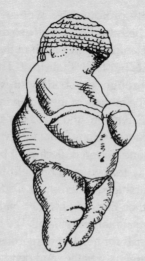

Figure 1—Venus of Willendorf, Austria

powers, and over time became elevated to the status of a god. In later years he was known to the Greeks as Pan, and to the Celts as Cernunnos. Today he is known loosely as the Horned God, and is one of the principle masculine deities invoked as consort to the Goddess in Neo-Pagan traditions.

As time went by and culture continued its inevitable evolution, the God and Goddess had children. What may have been nearly monotheistic Mother worship during Paleolithic times became polytheistic during the Neolithic period, with Gods and Goddesses of Sun and Moon, wind and rain, sowing and reaping, Heaven and Earth, and other

Figure 2—Dolni Vestonice,
Czechoslovakia

Figure 3—Venus of
Lespague, France

aspects of the natural world. Each culture had its
own pantheon with its own rites, but there were
similarities in the way they dissected the "Godhead" into the aspects of life and its cycles that
were important to the prospering of the people. As
population grew and travel connected diverse people, the older Gods and Goddesses, such as Isis or
the Horned One, became incorporated into many
pantheons with slight alterations. Thus the Goddess Inanna, of Sumerian mythology, was later
known as Ishtar to the Babylonians, Astarte to the
Canaanites, and Ashtoreth to the Hebrews.[2]

Among the archaeological remains throughout this entire period, from approximately 30,000 to 5,000 BCE (Before Common Era), there was one thing that was conspicuous by its absence: *war*. Warriors, weapons, scenes of battle, military fortifications, lavish burials of chieftains, evidence of slavery, or other hierarchical structures were simply not depicted in the art of these ancient peoples.[3] Instead, the art of cave paintings and sculpture abounds with nature symbols—Sun and earth, serpents and butterflies, bulls, birds, water and plants, as well as abundant images of the Goddess in her many forms. It is believed that this was a time of peace and cooperation between sexes, and between tribes. Indeed, life was difficult, and with high mortality rates, cooperation among members was the only way a tribe could survive.

This peaceful period began to erode around 5000 BCE with the invasion of patriarchal nomadic tribes, profoundly changing the course of the history of what we now consider the Western World. Most notable were the Kurgan invasions, starting at 4300 BCE and working their destruction in three basic waves, the first lasting 100 years, with 800 years until the next one from 3400–3200, and the last from 3000–2800 BCE. These people are also known as the light-skinned Aryans, who swarmed down from the European northeast, throughout Old Europe and India, in search of the warmer climates and fertile lands of the formerly prosperous civilizations. The Kurgan tribes were not alone however.

> As Aryans in India, Hittites and Mittani in the Fertile Crescent, Luwians in Anatolia, Kurgans in eastern Europe, Achaeans and later Dorians in Greece, they gradually impose their ideologies and ways of life on the lands and peoples they conquered.[4]

The invaders, which also included the Hebrews, brought with them their patriarchal gods of war. The peaceful birth-giving Earth Goddess was supplanted by the domination of fearful "creator" sky gods who demanded obeisance from the conquered people. And though they were of different races, origins, and time periods, the invaders shared one thing in common: *"a dominator model of social organization:* a social system in which male dominance, male violence, and a generally hierarchic and authoritarian social structure was the norm."[5] Their acquisition of wealth was based on technologies of destruction and conquering rather than on methods of production. With this came the domination of women and their sexuality, enabling the institution of patrilinear power structures and the ownership of private property. The conquering tribes killed the men, enslaved the women, and indoctrinated the children into the new system, took over the property and replaced the worship of local deities with the sky and war gods.

Despite these invasions and their deep alteration of the most advanced cultures at that time, Goddess worship continued to survive for several thousand more years. With the advent of writing, around 3,000 BCE, we have records that describe temples, rites, prayers and invocations to the Goddess in her many forms, providing us with a rich tapestry of mythology. In the fertile crescent, recently bombed during the Gulf War, the Goddess ruled strongly, where she evolved beyond a Nature deity to govern the rites of stateship. Yet even these later cultures had slavery and male domination, and the changing mythologies over the ensuing 3,000 years depict the gradual and often violent takeover by the patriarchal political systems as they exerted their power over religious practice. The Sumerian myth of Nergal and Ereshkigal's struggle in the Underworld, or the story of Persephone's abduction by Hades, are allegories of what happened to the Goddess during these periods.

The last stronghold of the Goddess, found in ancient Crete, was wiped out by 1100 BCE. How much of this was by natural catastrophe and how much by invading Acheaens, no one is quite sure, but Her open worship, with priestesses, temples, and public rites, came to an end. In Her cyclic nature, the Goddess began Her descent into the Underworld for a 3,000-year sleep of death.

Yet even in her sleep, the rural people of Europe still worshiped her in their seasonal rites of sowing and harvest, celebrating the dance of the Moon and Sun openly or in secret, passing their tradition down through families and communities. The religion of the land was hard to suppress for the farmers and shepherds who lived the rhythms of the land, but Goddess worship was no longer the rich and powerful tradition it once was, instead being broken up into isolated pockets of country folk practicing in fear and secrecy.

With the advent of Christianity, demanding loyalty to the church and the "One True God," the remains of the Pagan peoples and their practices were systematically suppressed by the ruling priesthood. As early as 430 CE (Common Era), heresy to the Christian church was punishable by death in some areas, though not enforced as frequently as it would be a millennium later.[6] Some Goddesses survived still, such as the Celtic Fire Goddess, Brigit, whose shrine at Kildare was tended by vestal virgins until 1220 CE, when it was finally denounced as a heathen custom by a Christian bishop.

And thus we come to the bitterest phase of Goddess history, for in 1227 began the Papal Inquisition, the start of 500 years of brutal thievery, torture, and murder of women and some men, who continued to worship the Goddess, practice healing and midwifery, and celebrate their seasonal, sacred rites. This was known as "the Burning Times," the persecution of the Witches, whose name comes from the Old English *wicce*, or wise ones. They were the teachers and healers, the herbalists and midwives, as well as the stubborn women and the men who supported them, by refusing to give up their personal power and freedom to the power-hungry Christian priesthood.

In 1486, two years after the first Papal Bull of Pope Innocent VIII, two German monks wrote a scathing manual, called the *Malleus Maleficarum*, for the identification and persecution of Witches. It was presented to the Theological Faculty at Cologne, who promptly rejected it. The monks forged the signatures and passed it through Europe, its forgery remaining undiscovered until 1898.[7] Through this document, the endorsement to burn and torture Witches was made official, and it is estimated that as many as 200,000 people, most of whom were women, were tortured for confessions, then burned at the stake or hung, followed by a confiscation of the family property of the deceased.[8]

It must be understood that, along with the violence, Christian usurpation took place by taking over many of the practices, holidays, sacred sites, and deities of the Pagan peoples. Churches were often constructed on Pagan holy ground. Holidays such as Christmas and Easter are carry-overs from the celebrations of the Pagan Yuletide and Ostara, or Spring rites (see **Holidays,** p. 29).

The Horned God, so firmly entrenched in Pagan theology for 30,000 years, was made into the Christian Devil—an instrument of evil. It is important to point out that the concept of a Devil had never existed in Pagan pantheons but was entirely a construction of Christian theology, as the shadow to the Christian God in a theology that divides creation into good and evil. Needing something to react against, the Devil became a motivating force of fear for Christians to move toward "moral behavior," something that seems extremely questionable considering the heinous crimes committed in the name of their new morality. Pagans, by contrast, have no Devil, and instead honor creation as an interpenetrating totality of constantly changing forces. Pagans see darkness as a time of rest, equivalent to the womb, the seed underground, or the peaceful period of death between lifetimes. While behavior that harms others is considered morally reprehensible, there are no archetypes of evil in Pagan mythology. Thus the view of Pagans as Devil worshippers, both historically and currently, is completely antithetical to all that Paganism stands for.

During the Burning Times, however, those who were arrested as practitioners of Witchcraft were usually tortured for confessions, and many told stories of cavorting with the Devil, under the duress of intense pain or the promise of freeing their families or friends. Hence, Paganism during the Burning Times was equated with Devil worship and brutally punished. The confessions were used by the Inquisitors to prove their point and further their savagery against the Pagan folk, building up their power through fear and their wealth through the confiscation of property.

The peak of the Witch burnings occurred from 1560–1660, and in 1604, King James passed the Elizabethan Witchcraft Act, proclaiming death by hanging for any form of witchcraft, or "consorting with the Devil." In America the famous Salem Witch trials were held in 1692, where 150 were accused and 31 condemned. The Elizabethan Act stayed in effect until 1736, when it was repealed under George II of England. At this time, Witchcraft was considered largely nonexistent, and those who professed to fortune-telling and such were charged with fraud and given a year in jail. Even so, isolated Witch burnings took place in France until 1745, and in Bavaria a Witch was beheaded as late as 1775.[9]

It is no wonder that Witchcraft became a thing of fantasy. During the height of the burnings, whole villages of 200 people or more could be executed—men, women, and children. Many had never had anything to do with Witchcraft of any kind but were merely prosperous farmers with property to lose. Others were certainly forewarned by the fate of their contemporaries to deeply bury any knowledge of practices they had—in fear for their very lives. To preserve one's life, it became necessary to completely deny knowledge of any existence of Witchcraft whatsoever, lest you, too, be considered a Witch and burned.

Fortunately, Witches believe in the cyclic nature of all life, making death an impermanent state. In 1921 information about Witchcraft and Pagan religions was to resurface through the writing of Margaret Murray in her book, *The Witch-Cult in Western Europe*. Here she proclaimed that Witchcraft had indeed existed as an organized religion with an unbroken line back to the cave people, a view that perhaps overstated the case but nonetheless brought the religion back out from the broom closet imposed by patriarchal monotheism. This paved the way for further research and a second book, *The God of the Witches*, published in 1931.

Finally, in 1951, the lingering laws against Witchcraft were repealed in England, granting a kind of amnesty to those who lived in fear and secrecy. Gerald Gardner, the founder of a branch of Wicca known as Gardnerian Witchcraft (see **Influences and Styles,** p. 35) came out publicly as a Witch, stating that Witchcraft was alive and well. His book, *Witchcraft Today* (1954), united practicing Witches throughout Europe in far greater numbers than any had suspected. In America, the first to come forth publicly was Raymond Buckland, to whose *Complete Book of Witchcraft* I can credit a good deal of the above history. In 1962, the first federally recognized Neo-Pagan organization, the Church of All Worlds, was founded by Tim (now Otter) Zell and Lance Christie, students at Westminster College in St. Louis. In 1969, Carl Weschcke of Llewellyn Publications hosted the first public gathering of Witches in the United States, the Gnostic Aquarian Festival, and the movement has grown exponentially ever since.

Though the recent history of Neo-Paganism centers largely around Wicca, or Witchcraft, it is by no means the only form practiced. The return to Native American shamanism reflects a similar belief system and style of worship, as do many forms of Buddhism and Hinduism, brought to us by the meeting of Eastern and Western religions that has blossomed during the last 30 years. Wicca is by and large the remnants of European shamanism, whereas the Native American tradition is the religion that rose from the spirits of American land.

The term *Neo-Pagan* is often used interchangeably with *Pagan* by its modern practitioners. The difference is that Neo-Paganism is a Renaissance movement, a reconstruction of ancient practices applied to the needs of an urban population, as distinguished from the ancient practices of ancestors, which have been all but lost during the millennia of suppression. Therefore Neo-Pagans must combine innovation and research in the recreation of their traditions. This gives modern Paganism a fresh perspective as well as an ancient tradition, making it simultaneously older and newer than any of the other major religions.

THEOLOGY, TRADITIONS, AND PRACTICES

Now that Neo-Paganism is re-emerging from its slumber, what form does it take? What is it that Neo-Pagans do? What are the fundamental beliefs of this religion? What do they worship and how?

The first and foremost cornerstone of Pagan belief systems is what is often called "the magical world view." More than a belief, it is an attitude toward the world around us, a fundamentally different perspective than any of the other major world religions. Neo-Pagans are highly individualistic people who prefer to think for themselves, shunning any prescribed dogma, so again, one "unified field theory" of Pagan belief systems is probably nonexistent. Yet there are some basic ideas that unite the many different paths through common principles. Some of these are as follows:

1. *Everything is connected to everything else.* On a direct level, this means that chemicals flushed into the river will float downstream and poison the fish in the ocean. On a deeper level, it states that animals and plants, social issues and environmental issues, thoughts, actions, and events, are all inter-

connected through an inseparable web of life. Anything that affects one part of the web will in some way affect all other parts. This includes connection between the planes of mind, body, and spirit. Therefore, our actions, conscious or not, have an effect on the world around us. Pagans choose, through ritual, to make conscious the connection between self and environment, action and event.

2. *Everything is cyclic.* Pagans do not view their lives, their events, their world, or its social structures on a linear time frame. As the Earth is round, and the seasons repeat again and again, everything is seen as a spiral of cyclic energy. Death is the rest and recuperation that precedes rebirth and is a necessary stage for any movement or life form to continue indefinitely. Neo-Pagans see the world as having natural limits that must be respected and do not support uncontrolled growth, population, or use of natural resources. Thus a fertile field should be allowed to remain fallow every few years to maintain its ongoing fertility. The cycles of nature form the fundamental basis for the seasonal and lunar rituals and celebrations as well as for the stages of human life, the beginning and ending of projects, and the rise and fall of political empires.

3. *Nature knows best.* Pagans see the Earth as a living Deity, a planetary being that is conscious,

and self-regulating. Our "scripture" is in the bio-sphere, in biology and geology, zoology and botany—the natural cycles of growth and life and death. While we believe in personal empowerment through individual will, we seek to align our will with the greater will of the planet and the deities that we worship. In all that we do, natural laws have the highest respect and provide the moral foundation for personal and cultural behavior. Thus it is morally reprehensible to leave litter in the forest, to waste resources unnecessarily, or to cause avoidable pain or harm to another living creature, human or otherwise. The animal kingdom is seen as part of the family of living creatures, no less important than humans.

4. *Deity is immanent.* From the roots of animism, pantheism, and polytheism, this means that deity exists *in* everything—within each one of us, within the plants, the animals, the rocks, the mountains, the Sun and Moon and the stars beyond. The expression, "Thou Art God, Thou Art Goddess," reminds Neo-Pagans of the incredible responsibility of carrying the divine within. What we do to ourselves, we do to the God and Goddess. If we abuse or pollute ourselves, each other, the Earth, or the animals, we are abusing divinity itself.

5. *Paganism is polytheistic, with special honor to the Goddess.* Pagans believe that the Gods and spir-

its come in many forms, from ancient deities of cosmic proportion, such as the Egyptian star goddess, Nut, to the small and local nature spirits, such as faeries and plant devas, who inhabit the groves, streams, springs, and meadows of the natural world. Fundamental to Paganism is the recognition of deity in a female form. In most cases, the feminine deity is not in exclusion to the male form but is usually given priority, due to the tremendous imbalance between male and female god forms over the last 5,000 years.

The Goddess represents the Divine Feminine, present in all women, in the fertile Earth, the Moon and its cycles, all material forms, and many nonmaterial concepts. She is Queen of Heaven, Mistress of the Underworld, Mother Earth, Sister Moon. She is the ultimate mystery, always inviting one to probe deeper, never to be fully revealed. She is the temple of the body, the manifested form, which we are all privileged to experience, and to hold as sacred. She is pleasure and joy, unconditional love, power and wisdom. She is seen as the basic field upon which all life is played. She is creatress by virtue of Her ability to give birth; nurturer by Her ability to sustain life, emotionally and physically; and destroyer by Her natural limits that bring us all, eventually, to death.

Like the Christian Godhead, She is seen in triplicity, and Her three aspects are called the Maiden, the Mother, and the Crone. The Maiden relates to young women from their first blood until they have children, and rules over the springtime, youth, innocence, beauty, passion, and purity. The Mother relates to the phase of a woman's life that is involved with birthing and raising children (or projects, for those who choose to remain childless) and She rules over summer and fall, as well as conception, birth, marriage, prosperity, nurturance, healing, and growth. The Crone relates to the third part of a woman's life, after menses stop, when the children have left home. The Crone represents wisdom and rules over the winter months, through teaching, meditation, disintegration of old habits, hard lessons, and the rest that comes from our final death.

Because Goddess worship was so brutally suppressed, and because there is still so little of it in the world today, the Goddess is generally given greater importance than the God. Thus the Priestess in a Pagan circle will usually have final say over the Priest, the Goddess is generally addressed before the God, and the feminine is highly honored in both women and men, seen as a basic fundamental value. Therefore women in Neo-Paganism find personal inspiration in a feminine deity—for the Goddess within gives reason to treat oneself with respect and honor and restores a sense of dignity. The men in Neo-Paganism are equally happy with this concept, for they have strong women who take pride in what they are, who have no need to live vicariously through their men. A happy woman, steeped in her own inner divine power, has more to give, more potency in what she creates, and more self-reliance. Sexuality is celebrated as a holy act, with passion and power, yet women's boundaries are also respected, allowing maidens to choose their own time to make love or have children, and allowing mothers the freedom of choice over their reproductive capacities. Honoring the feminine gives men permission to break away from stereotyped male behavior and search more deeply and honestly for their own definition of self.

The Goddess is not omnipotent, however, nor is She an abstract concept that exists "out there." She can be harmed, as we are presently harming the form of the Goddess that we know as Mother Earth. The Goddess has limits, as well as deep reserves of strength and mystery. She is the archetypal force behind the real and material, the everyday field of love and emotions, death and birth. She is in everything, and She is always there. Worship of Her strengthens Her field of influence, strengthens the feminine balance in the world, and restores women and Nature to the realm of the Sacred.

Counterpart and consort to the Goddess, the God is a potent entity in His own right. Seen as the influence that inspires the Goddess to evolve and change, the God is the driving force that initiates, ignites, and catalyzes. In triplicity, He is Youth,

Father, and Sage, although these aspects are not as strongly stressed in the God because they are less biologically marked in men's lives. Instead He is Lover and Protector, Warrior and Teacher, Father and Ruler. He is the Dancer, while the Goddess is the Dance. He is the flame, the Goddess is the Fire. He is the Holy part of the male psyche, King and Priest, Comforter and Consoler. While embracing the old pre-Christian archetypes of the God, many Neo-Pagan men are also working to evolve new archetypes that bring honor to themselves and the world around them—archetypes that fit the changing role of men in a world working for peace and equality between the sexes.

Existing archetypes are many. As the Horned One, He is God of the animal kingdom, of love, joy, and sexuality, and protector of the forest and of the Craft. As the Green Man, He is seen as a cyclic energy that dies and is reborn. As the Green Man is God of growing things, He is sacrificed each year in the form of wheat, corn, or other vegetation. Yet He returns each year in Spring to renew us all once more. His sacrifice is honored and the miracle of His return is cause to rejoice. While human sacrifice, practiced at times by the ancients, would be considered unthinkable to any modern Neo-Pagan, symbolic personal sacrifices, such as giving up a food or a habit, or offering of a gift, may be used instead. It is recognized through the dance of the God that we all must make certain sacrifices to achieve our ends.

We sacrifice time and money to go to school, we sacrifice freedom to have children, we sacrifice eating in order to fast on a vision quest. The God reminds us to give thanks for what we have, for our food, the animals that sacrificed their lives for our dinner, for the grain that makes our bread.

The God is also the Sun and the sky that penetrate the field of the Earth and enable life to exist. At Winter Solstice, for example, we celebrate the return of the Sun God in the form of a new-born child. He is also the cunning trickster that keeps us on our toes, as in the form of Loki, the Norse God of Fire, or Hanuman, the Hindu Monkey God. As Warrior, he inspires strength and protection, power and pride. Men who worship the God in His many forms need not fear women in their power.

Together, the God and the Goddess form the interpenetrating duality that is the constant field of creation. All aspects of our known universe are represented, birth and death, dark and light, Heaven and Earth, male and female. Each is complete within itself, yet each completes the other. The Goddess exists within men as well as women, just as the God is within both women and men. They are the archetypal duality, the eternal Dance of Life. Their ways of worship are many, but their most basic honoring comes through the simple recognition of their presence within each other and within all things. Thou Art God. Thou Art Goddess.

6. *Ethics:* Pagan ethics are grounded in an ancient maxim: "If it harm none, do what you will." It is believed that it only harms oneself to harm another, and all deeds react upon the doer threefold. If we are all part of an interconnected web, of which all parts are the Goddess, then all harmful actions are crimes against the deity, whether they are acts against self, other, or environment. Pagans do not believe in a concept of "sin and forgiveness," but instead see things in terms of cause and effect, sometimes called karma. If harm has been caused, amends must be made in order to heal the breach in the greater web. This is an act of conscience, of personal responsibility, of ongoing connection with the divine. Where harm does not occur, Pagans believe in allowing people privacy and freedom for their own actions. Within this framework, small acts must be weighed against larger effects, such as a woman's decision to end a pregnancy, where the decision to terminate is weighed against the effects of the potential harm in raising a child without proper emotional and physical support, and contributing in this way to overpopulation, poverty, and potential child abuse.

7. *Personal Empowerment.* Pagans believe in that indefinable experience that we call Magic (often spelled Magick, to distinguish it from the tricks of stage magicians). Magick is defined in many ways, depending on one's tradition. Some of the most common are:

The art of causing change in conformity with will.

The art of causing a change in consciousness as a result of intention.

The art of coincidence control, or probability enhancement.

The art of transformation.

Neo-Pagans believe that they have the power to change the circumstances around them, whether it be lack of a job, healing from an illness, or the gradual restoration of balance to the planet as a whole. Along with personal empowerment comes personal responsibility. If we can affect the world around us by our very thoughts and actions, then we need to be extremely conscious of all that we do. This can include everything from recycling our garbage, to how we treat the beggar on the street, to what we do within our ceremonies.

8. *Earth, water, fire, and air.* Pagans honor the four directions (north, west, south, and east) through correspondence with the four basic elements, the four building blocks of all life, or what Starhawk calls the "Four Sacred Things." The elements are associated with aspects of our experience, such as the earth which brings us grounding and stability, the water which brings us healing

and soothing, the fire which gives us energy, and the air which gives us clarity. Some traditions may work with a fifth element of spirit.

9. *Neo-Pagans are non-hierarchical.* Generally speaking, Neo-Pagans shun the idea of hierarchy in the form of gurus, masters, or a separate priesthood set off from the rest of population. There are both priests and priestesses in Pagan circles, but the job may rotate among its members from month to month, or year to year.

There are more organizations now instituting ordination procedures for those who feel a calling to make Priesthood a life dedication. This is seen as a commitment to service rather than a position of power. Pagans do not see a priest or priestess as a necessary intermediary between themselves and deity, finding the experience to be direct and personal. A priest or priestess may, however, *represent* the deity in a ceremony, and agree to channel that energy to the participants in the ceremony. This act of linking can be done by anyone with adequate training, and is not relegated to a separate class.

Those who are ordained as Pagan clergy make it their life commitment and are equally busy with administrative tasks, counseling, teaching, and grunt work, such as collating newsletters, chopping wood, or typesetting articles.

10. *The Circle.* Pagan worship occurs with participants and celebrants together in a circle, outdoors whenever possible. The circularity allows all participants to interact within a format of basic equality. The ritual formation of the circle creates a container for the energy, marks the ritual space as sacred, and signifies the beginning and, by its dismissal, the end of a rite. The holding of rites outdoors helps to increase connection with the natural world.

While public gatherings may hold rites for large numbers of people (100–1,000 at a time), most Pagan circles are small and intimate. The ideal number for an ongoing group of Witches who work together (called a coven) is said to be 13, representing the 13 Moons of the year. This also enables groups to have intimacy and creativity, to fit in someone's living room or between the trees in a grove, and to keep ceremonies simple and personal. Other open circles may range from 5 to 50, depending on the group.

11. *Neo-Pagans have a positive attitude about their bodies and about sexuality.* Sexuality is seen as a sacred act of God and Goddess uniting. The needs and feelings of the body are not something to overcome but something to enjoy and celebrate. Pagans may express their sexuality in many different ways, from heterosexual monogamy to bisexual

polygamy, including a large faction of gay and lesbian worshippers. It is a myth that Pagans have numerous secret orgies in their rituals, though many holidays, such as Beltane (May 1) feature sexuality between the Goddess and the God in a symbolic way, and the practice of sex magic may occur between couples or in smaller groups for specific purposes.

12. *Cycles.* Neo-Pagan worship occurs in conjunction with the cycles of the Moon and the Sun. Covens and smaller circles meet on the new and/or Full Moon. Anyone who lives in the woods can sense the heightened activity of the forest during the Full Moon, and in ancient times it provided light for our ancestors as they traveled through the wood to their meetings. Today we see the Full Moon as a time of beauty and a peaking of feminine power.

HOLIDAYS

There are eight major solar holidays in the Pagan calendar. They occur at the Solstices and Equinoxes and the cross-quarter days between them. The holidays have specific significance in what is called the *Wheel of the Year*, or the cyclic journey of balance that we undergo in each year's trip around the Sun. The holidays form the foundation for what remains of ancient Pagan traditions, the symbols and meanings commemorated in ritual year after year. How these symbols are expressed, however, is open to creative innovation and may vary from group to group.

Samhain. (pronounced sow-onn). October 31– November 7

This is the Celtic New Year signified by the death of the old year, when the harvest is in, the plants are going underground for the winter, and the veil is thinnest between our mundane world and the worlds of spirit. Known popularly as All Hallow's Eve, or Halloween, this is the time of year for honoring our ancestors and those who are dear to us who have passed away. In ritual they are honored by speaking their names, or making an altar for their pictures, for it is said, "What is remembered, lives." At this time we face the approaching darkness of the winter by turning inward and focusing on our visions, our dreams, our meditation and study. This is also a time for turning a new leaf, allowing our negative habits to enter the realm of death.

Yule. December 21

The longest and darkest night of the year is honored by sharing stories around the Yule log, often keeping a vigil until the light of the new Sun returns in the morning. Between Samhain and Yule is the period of mourning, of letting things go. Yule is the pivot point of the year, the return to hope through welcoming the light that begins to increase at that time. Similar to the Christian Christmas, Pagans worship the rebirth of the Sun King, as the child of promise, and also exchange gifts, sing carols, and celebrate festively.

Brigit, Candlemas, Imbolc, or Lady's Day. February 1–7

This is the time of the quickening, when the light gains in strength and warmth, and the earliest plants begin to push up out of the ground. In conjunction with the increased warmth, it is often dedicated to Brigit, the Celtic Fire Goddess. Celebrations for Brigit may include a sharing of poetry written during the reflective time of the winter, prayers for healing, protection and blessings for the children, and the lighting of numerous candles to welcome and bring back the light.

Ostara, or Spring Equinox. March 21

Ostara is a time of balance and promise. The soil may be soft enough to plant in some climates. Trees begin to bud. The famous Easter Egg hunts we associate with the Christian holiday are actually an old Pagan rite of *Ostara Eggs*, where the egg was the symbol of the birth that was about to be witnessed in the ensuing weeks. Wishes were made upon the eggs for the coming growing season, or for the granting of personal needs. This is a time of celebrating the balance of light and dark and the joyous approach of springtime.

Beltane. April 30–May 7

Beltane is the time of flowering—a passage into the light of summer. It is the celebration of adolescence, sexuality, and fertility, where the Maiden aspect of the Goddess mates with the animal aspect of the God, ensuring potency and fertility for the growing season. Sexuality is celebrated symbolically by dancing around a Maypole, representing male potency grounded in the Earth Mother. Dancing upon the Earth is believed to awaken the soil from winter's slumber and ensure an abundant growing season. As it is a mating day for the Gods, it is a particularly auspicious time to conceive a child.

Summer Solstice, or Litha. June 20, 21

Summer Solstice is the high point of the year, the brightest point on the wheel, when the Sun is at its zenith and the joyful aspects of light, life, and love are celebrated. The adolescent time of Beltane reaches a greater maturity, the Youth and Maiden turn to Mother and Father, with children, budding crops, and wildlife to care for. The holiday may be celebrated with a sacred bonfire, whose flames bring luck and energize the crops, by sprinkling ashes from the fire on the garden.

Lammas, or Lughnasad. August 1-7

Lammas is the time of first fruits, and its name literally means loaf-mass, being the time when the very first bit of grain from the harvest can be baked into a loaf and shared. This is the beginning of the harvest season, and the beginning of the time of cutting, thinning, setting limits, and turning once again toward the coming darkness. It is also called Lughnasadh, in honor of the Celtic Fire God, Lugh, who battles with Balor for the change from a waxing Sun to a waning Sun.

Mabon, or Fall Equinox. September 21, 22

A time of balance between dark and light, this is a time of celebrating and sharing the harvest, and preparing for the descent into the approaching darkness of winter. In ancient times, the harvest was a demanding time of hard work, bringing in the food and firewood in preparation for the colder months ahead. Today it is a time of focusing one's energy after the summer months and reaping the harvest of one's work through the year. Usually accompanied by a large feast, it is a time of giving thanks and working for prosperity.

This then brings us back again to Samhain, the year's final end and new beginning, and thus the cycle continues once again, ever as a spiral turning and evolving with each passing year.

The eight major solar holidays of the year correspond to stages of growth in the life cycle of human, plant, organization, or project. The stages of conception, gestation, birth, growth, maturation, and death are reflected in the ever-changing spiral of the year, and the correspondences of the holidays are used to aid us in working through any of these stages. Within the cycles described by these holidays are shorter cycles of the Moon's waxing and waning, the diurnal cycle of day and night, and the varied cycles of the other planets whose aspects may have an effect upon us.

Some traditions even have tables of planetary hours and their associations, so that one might choose, for example, to do prosperity magic on a Thursday, during an hour associated with the planet Jupiter. Other workings may correspond to the monthly Moon cycles, using the waxing Moon as a time to work for the increase of something, like business activity, and a waning Moon as a time to help decrease something, such as removing excess weight or quitting smoking. Esbats, as Moon-related rituals are often called, may also be coordinated to the Zodiac sign the Moon is in, as well as the phase of the Moon, just as planting and harvesting may also be coordinated to "Moon signs" to enhance the plants' growth and production. Thus all magical work is aligned with the greater cycles of the Earth and the Heavens.

INFLUENCES AND STYLES

Like Christianity, with its subdivisions of Catholic and Protestant, and the many widely differing Protestant denominations, Neo-Paganism comes in many flavors and styles. The following is an attempt to describe the major influences and contemporary styles that make up the larger body of the Neo-Pagan community. It is by no means exhaustive, for Neo-Pagans pride themselves on the the diversity of their ways, and many groups are eclectic blends of several of the traditions listed below.

Wicca, or Witchcraft

This is a major subheading, whose generic meaning has been described above. It is a branch of resurrected European shamanism, combining folkloric customs from many cultures, revering a God and Goddess as divine couple, worshiping the power of nature as the Goddess, Mother Earth, and empowering the individual to make change through psychic and ritual techniques. Subcategories of Witchcraft include (but are not limited to) the following branches:

Gardnerian Witchcraft—Founded in the 1950s by the Englishman, Gerald Gardner (1884–1964), Gardnerian Witchcraft is probably the most widely practiced craft system among contemporary Neo-

Pagans. Based on rituals inherited and created by Gardner and one of his coveners, Doreen Valiente, Gardnerian Witchcraft honors the polarity of male and female, with emphasis on the Goddess, the four directions, the Moon cycle, and the eight solar holidays. This tradition is practiced in covens of 13 or less, who work skyclad (naked) and strive to have a balance of men and women. There are three levels of initiation, and both teaching and initiation flow from male to female or from female to male. Covens are led by a High Priestess, who must be at least a third-degree initiate.

Alexandrian Wicca—An outgrowth of Gardnerian Witchcraft, this branch was founded by Alex Sanders (1926–1988), another English contemporary of Gerald Gardner, who used the same type of rituals but put more emphasis on ceremonial magic.

Seax Wica—Founded by Raymond Buckland, who brought Gardnerian Wicca to the United States, Seax Wica has a Saxon basis. It differs from Gardnerian in that rituals are open, practice can occur in covens or solitary, skyclad or robed, and the organization is pointedly democratic.

Fam Trads—"Fam trads" is the popular way of referring to a tradition a practitioner may have inherited from her or his family. There is no list of particular traditions, but rather sets of practices one may have learned from mother, father, or grandmother that are more indigenous to the folk religion of the country of ancestry. In rare cases, fam trads may boast an unbroken line of tradition to early witchcraft, kept secret through the generations until it was safe to share them openly. In fam trads, initiation usually occurs through a family member.

Dianic—There are two main branches of Dianic Witchcraft. Originally founded in the late 60s by Morgan McFarland and Mark Roberts, it was a tradition practiced by both men and women, focusing especially on the Goddesss Diana, a Greek nature deity, with a strong feminist slant. Later, Z Budapest, a feminist Witch claiming a Hungarian fam trad, brought Dianic Witchcraft to the women's movement, where it became a women-only tradition focusing on the Goddess alone. Some Dianic covens are exclusively lesbian, while others may include lesbian, bisexual, and heterosexual women. Dianics believe that exclusive focus on the Goddess is necessary to balance the heavy patriarchal elements of our current culture.

Faerie—Faerie tradition is a branch of Wicca founded by Victor Anderson that combines Celtic myth and practice with Huna traditions of the Hawaiian Islands. Faerie tradition works with the sensual elements of sight, sound, and smell, with heavy emphasis on visualization. Also emphasized are the forces of unseen nature spirits, and the entrance into ecstatic states of unity with the inner subconscious and with the natural world. Many noteworthy elders in the Neo-Pagan community were initiated in Faerie tradition.

Radical Faeries—The Radical Faeries are a tradition, largely of gay men (though not exclusively), who focus on redefining the masculine and honoring the feminine. Strongly political and nature oriented, the Radical Faeries overlap with other Pagan groups as well as having a close-knit subcommunity.

Traditions Outside of Witchcraft

Feraferia—Founded by Frederick McLaren Adams, Feraferia is a Greco-Roman mystery tradition inspired by the writings of Robert Graves, author of The *White Goddess* and the novel *Watch the North Wind Rise*. Nature-oriented, with special focus on the rituals of the changing seasons, Feraferia was seminal to the early Neo-Pagan reformation.

Norse Paganism—This branch of Neo-paganism works with the deities of Norse mythology and stresses the values of courage, honor, and duty to one's lineage and community. The rekindling of Norse practices sprang up in the early 70s and has further subsets, which may focus on the two main branches of Gods, the Aesir and the Vanir. The Aesir are basically the Sky Gods, such as Odin and Frigga, Thor, Loki, etc. The Vanir are connected with Earth and agricultural cycles. Most followers of Norse Paganism worship both sets, with the exception of Odinism, which worships only the Aesir. The warrior aspect is a strong flavor in Norse mythology, and while some may say it is male dominated, females find archetypes of strong women warriors equally appealing, and claim that the Goddesses of Norse Paganism have been given short shrift by historians but are fundamental to the religion.

Because Norse Paganism uses symbols that were usurped by Hitler and the Nazi Party, such as the swastika, many Norse practitioners are accused of being Neo-Nazi. While a few right-wing groups do exist, they are not considered a part of the Neo-Pagan community and are generally excluded by other Norse worshippers.

The *Ring of Troth* is an organization dedicated to the promotion and preservation of the Northern European folk religion and made up of people who come together for cultural and religious reasons, rather than for racial and political reasons. One of their central texts is *A Book of Troth* (Llewellyn, 1989), written by Edred Thorsson, who founded the organization in 1987, but resigned in 1991 and passed it on to Prudence Priest. They publish a scholarly quarterly magazine, *Idunna*, a sample copy of which is available for $7 from The Troth,

PO Box 18812, Austin TX 78760, or free with membership ($24/year single, $33 family).

Other Cultural Flavors—There are groups that may choose to focus on a particular culture or pantheon, such as Celtic, Middle Eastern, Egyptian, Greek, Oceanic, Oriental, Hindu, or Tibetan Buddhist. These may or may not be mixed with other, modern traditions. Because of the emphasis on diversity, and the recognition that the melting pot of the Americas makes all cultures part of our ancestry, most groups borrow heavily and combine any of the traditions listed herein.

Druidism—The Druid branch of Neo-Paganism, largely spearheaded by Isaac Bonewits, is a reconstruction of the ancient Celtic oral tradition. Druids of old were the teachers, the Bards (musicians), the scholars, and the traveling Priests who spread knowledge of traditional wisdom, theology, and moral philosophy throughout the Celtic lands from perhaps as early as the 5th century BCE until the 4th century CE, not to be revived again until the 16th and 17th centuries. They were of the higher classes and were skilled in divination, herbal medicine, ritual implementation, astronomy, the construction of calendars, music, and poetry.

Today Druidism is alive in Europe and the United States. Until recently, English Druids held ceremonies at Stonehenge, a megalithic monument that was once believed to have been built by the Druids, though modern theories refute this. British Druidism is said to have been revived in 1717 by William Stukeley and John Tolan, and revised by the Masons.

In 1965, students at Carleton College in Minnesota founded a Druid order, RDNA (Reformed Druids of North America). It began as a hoax to protest a school requirement to attend religious services, but they soon became so fascinated by the religion that they began to set up an organization of Druid "groves." They joined with the Neo-Pagan movement through NRDNA, or New Reformed Druids of North America, led by ArchDruid Isaac Bonewits, author of *Real Magic*. Later, in 1983, Isaac founded another organization, still active today, called *Ar nDraiocht Fein (ADF)*, which translates as "our own Druidism." ADF focuses on scholarship and training, with emphasis on healing, ecological awareness, music, and liturgy.

A split-off from ADF, *Celtria*, focuses more on the Wiccan side of Celtic mythology, and is an initiatory tradition.

Huna—A Hawaiian shamanic system working especially with the three aspects of the soul—upper, middle, and lower, Huna was popularized in this country by the writings of Max Freedom Long and was an influence in Victor Anderson's creation of the *Faery Tradition*.

Santería, Umbanda—Santería brings forth a true unbroken tradition from Africa, worshipping ancient African Gods, some of whom have been assimilated as Catholic saints. (The word comes from *santo,* or saint.) Santería comes from the Yoruban tribes along the Niger River in West Africa. When millions of slaves were brought to this country in Spanish ships, they brought with them their religion. Being forced by their Spanish masters to convert to Catholicism, they gradually syncretized the two faiths, and practitioners of Santería abound in Hispanic-Catholic cultures as well as Afro-American.

The gods of the Santería religion, called *orishas,* have complex personalities and can be called upon to enter the body of the practitioners through a conscious seeking of possession states. The focus of Santería is knowledge and relationship with the orishas, divination, and healing, especially through herbalism.

Umbanda is the Brazilian form of Santería and differs in that it may embrace a wider spectrum of practices, such as including Buddhist or Hindu influences. The name is from the Portuguese and means "one group."

Voudoun—The word *voudoun* relates to *vodu* or "spirit, deity," and can be traced to the language of the Dahomey kingdom in Nigeria.[10] The uninformed may mistakenly call it "voodoo," but the term is generally considered pejorative. It flourishes most strongly in Haiti, but also in New

Orleans, New York, Houston, and Charleston, South Carolina. Like Santería, Voudoun came to this world through the African slaves. And like Witchcraft, slaves who practiced their native religion were sadistically punished, including mutilation, sexual disfigurement, flaying, burying alive, imprisonment, or hanging.[11] Like the *orishas,* Voudoun has a set of gods called *loas,* the father of which is the Great Serpent, or Danbhalah-Wedo. Contact with the loas occurs through possession, and rites involve drumming and dancing and the building of altars, and may include animal sacrifice.

Hinduism—Practitioners of Hinduism are beginning to join forces with the Neo-Pagan community because they have discovered so many Neo-Pagans worshipping their gods and goddesses. There are many commonalities of beliefs, as well as a multiplicity of deities, most of whom come in pairs of divine couples, such as Brahma and Saraswati, creators; Vishnu and Laksmi, preservers; and Shiva and Kali, destroyers. Hindu gods are frequently invoked in Neo-Pagan circles, and in India these gods have living traditions, temples, and unbroken lines of worship through history.

Tantra, a further subcategory of Hinduism, is focused on the divine union of male and female through sexuality and sensuality. In Tantra, a practitioner regards the body as a sacred temple, and believes that, through practicing certain yogas of sexual union, one can achieve experiences of kundalini arousal, awakening of the chakras, and higher states of consciousness.

Tibetan Buddhism—There are enough Neo-Pagans simultaneously involved with Eastern religions to have coined the term, Buddheo-Pagan. While some forms of Buddhism may imply rigorous self-denial and withdrawal from the worlds, other aspects are extremely polytheistic, honoring Goddesses as well as Gods. Buddheo-Pagans contribute the threads of deep meditation; philosophical constructs, such as the Bodhisattva, who work for the enlightenment of all sentient beings; and the power of compassion and prayer. Tibetan deities also have a time-honored tradition of uninterrupted worship.

Ceremonial Magick—Ceremonial magick is a branch of Neo-Paganism that differs from generic Witchcraft in the formality and precision of its rituals. Many consider it more of a practice than a religion, being less focused on theology and more on the influences of cause and effect. Using a more intellectual approach, the ceremonial magician sets up rituals based on elaborate symbolism of numbers, colors, tools, timing, and movement. Ceremonial magick focuses heavily on concentration and will, and may employ the Jewish Tree of Life of the

Qaballah (or Kaballah) as a working model. The Tree of Life is a system of ten Sephiroth, or spheres, which represent ten areas of consciousness and/or cosmic reality, ranging from Malkuth, the base which represents the manifested kingdom, to Kether, the Crown, and beyond to the creative limitless light, the eternal source of creation.

Three groups practicing ceremonial magick today are the Aurum Solis, the Golden Dawn, and the O.T.O.

Native American Shamanism—In recent years, there has been a wide resurgence of interest and practice in Native American traditions. As people are searching for a back-to-the-land religion, many are finding connection with a religion that is indigenous to North American soil. Commonalities with Pagan worship have brought Native American customs, chants, and rituals into Neo-Pagan circles, such as the common use of "smudging," which is to mark Sacred Space by inhaling the incense from a burning piece of sage, cedar, or sweetgrass. Drumming circles are common in Native American traditions, as are vision quests, fasts, and ritual chanting. All these customs are also common in Neo-Pagan practices.

Native American elders have mixed feelings about the overlap with Neo-Paganism. Many feel that white Europeans have been "stealing" from Native Americans since they arrived 500 years ago, and the use and possible misuse of their traditions, as well as the many high-priced seminars in Shamanic Journeying or Medicine Ways, are just another example of the white man exploiting their culture. Others (Hopis, for example) feel that it has long been prophesied that a generation will come that will remember Indian ways and ask for teachings so that they can return to them.

CONCLUSION

Neo-Paganism is a religion that is alive and thriving. Its rituals are meaningful, passionate, colorful, and fun. Its philosophies are relevant to today's world as well as being deeply embedded in the past. It works with both the conscious and the unconscious, with rich symbolism, ecstatic music and drumming, colorful costumes, and potent archetypal images. It is a religion that honors the individual as a carrier of the divine, and honors the world we live in as equally divine. It is a religion that answers to the needs of our time—the environmental crises, the loss of faith and purpose, and the emptiness and despair within so many individuals and society. It is a religion with a strong sense of community, forged perhaps by centuries of persecution, but supported by common purpose, mutual respect, and the sharing of joy.

These few pages have illustrated the basic conceptual building blocks of Pagan religion, yet have barely scratched the surface of a highly complex mythological world view. In the words of a fellow Pagan priest, this is "a religion that we are simultaneously remembering and inventing together."[12] There is little that is simple, and as a constantly growing and evolving religion, there is also very little that is absolute. Change itself is the basis upon which magick is built. Neo-Paganism is an old religion for a new age—a time-honored tradition being rebirthed in a very different world from the one in which it originated. As an experientially oriented spirituality, the only way to truly grasp the magic and mystery is to get involved and experience it for yourself. And may all who enter with an open heart, recognizing their kinship with all that lives, be welcome.[13]

MAJOR ORGANIZATIONS

Ar nDriaocht Fein (ADF) (Druid)
PO Box 1022, Nyack NY 10960

Aurum Solis (Ceremonial Magick)
BCM Tessera, London WC1N 3XX, England

Bay Area Pagan Assemblies (BAPA) (Pagan Eclectic)
PO Box 850, Fremont CA 94537
Central Florida Council of Covens (Wiccan)
PO Box 2587, Bellview FL 32620

Church of All Worlds (Pagan Eclectic)
PO Box 1542, Ukiah CA 95482
Church of All Worlds has numerous Nests nation-
wide and publishes the foremost Pagan journal,
Green Egg. Write for information on subscriptions
or on Nests in your area.

Church of Y Tylwyth Teg (Celtic)
PO Box 674884, Marietta GA 30067

Circle of Aradia, Ruth Barrett, (Dianic Women)
41111 Lincoln Blvd. #211, Marina Del Rey CA 90292

Circle Sanctuary (Pagan Eclectic—Networking)
PO Box 219, Mt. Horeb WI 53572

Council of the Blue Moon (Women Only)
PO Box 27465, San Antonio TX 78227

Covenant of the Goddess (COG) (Generic Wiccan)
Formed in 1975, a national organization designed to
foster relations among various covens and solitaries,
as well as provide protection against harassment,
and recognition of Witchcraft as a legitimate religion.
PO Box 1226, Berkeley CA 94704

Earth Spirit Community (Pagan Eclectic)
PO Box 365, Medford MA 02155

Fellowship of the Spiral Path (Pagan Eclectic)
Box 5521, Berkeley CA 94705
Feraferia
PO Box 314, Pacific Grove CA 93950

The Georgian Church (Largely Gardnerian)
1908 Verde St., Bakersfield CA 93304

Golden Dawn (Ceremonial Magick)
There are many organizations operating in the tradition of the Hermetic Order of the Golden Dawn, founded in 1887 in Victorian England by W. Wynn Westcott, W. R. Woodman, and MacGregor Mathers. One of them is:

Ra-Horakhty Temple
Hermetic Society of the Golden Dawn
31849 Pacific Hwy. South, Suite 107, Federal Way
    WA 980034

Another good resource for Golden Dawn information is:
Chic Cicero and Sandra Tabatha Cicero
PO Box 1757, Elfers FL 34680–1757

Heartland Pagan Association (Pagan Eclectic)
2237 West Morse Ave., Chicago IL 60645

Keltria (Celtic Druid)
PO Box 33284, Minneapolis MN 55433

Midwest Pagan Council
PO Box 313, Matteson IL 60443

Mother Hearth (Women Only)
c/o Spider, 222 Rad Nor Ave., Pittsburgh PA 15221

Northern Way (Norse)
Nova Coven, 45 S. La Vergne Ave., Northlake IL
60164

Of A Like Mind (Women Only), publishes newsletter
PO Box 6021, Madison WI 53716

Ordo Templi Orientis (Ceremonial Magick)
A magical order once headed by Aleister Crowley, being primarily of the Ceremonial Magick flavor. Its practitioners are called Thelemites, and there are nine degrees of initiation. The O.T.O. is an outgrowth of the Masons, originally founded in Germany and supposedly descended from the Knights Templar. There are various organizations claiming to be the legitimate heir of Crowley's O.T.O., but the largest in the United States, with chapters throughout the U.S. and Europe, is:
Ordo Templi Orientis
PO Box 2303, Berkeley CA 94702

Pagans In Recovery (a self-help network for addiction recovery, with newsletter)
22 Palmer St., Athens OH 45701, (614) 664–5050

The Pallas Society (Generic Wiccan)
PO Box 18211, Encino CA 01316

Reclaiming (Political Pagan)
PO Box 14404, San Francisco CA 94114

Ring of Troth (Northern European)
PO Box 18812, Austin TX 78760

Witches Anti-Defamation League (Political Pagan)
153 W. 80th St. #1B, New York NY 10024

Witches League for Public Awareness (Political Pagan)
PO Box 8736, Salem MA 01971

Women's Spirituality Forum, Z Budapest (Dianic,
woman identified)
PO Box 11363, Oakland CA 94611

Universal Federation of Pagans (Networking)
An organization uniting a large number of diverse
groups
PO Box 674884, Marietta GA 30067

This listing represents only a very few of the
hundreds of Neo-Pagan organizations presently in
existence. For further information, contact **Circle** at
the above address for their *Circle Guide to Pagan
Resources*.

FOOTNOTES

1. Marija Gimbutas, *The Goddesses and Gods of Old Europe: Myths and Cult Images,* University of California Press, 1982, p. 11.

2. Ashtoreth was a mistranslation, and means shameful one, due to the prominent sexuality of the goddess. Patricia Monaghan, *The Book of Goddesses and Heroines,* Llewellyn Publications, 1981, p. 38.

3. Riane Eisler, *The Chalice and the Blade,* Harper & Row, 1987, pp. 17–18.

4. Eisler, p. 44

5. Eisler, p. 45

6. Rosemary Guiley, *Encyclopedia of Witches and Witchcraft,* Facts-on-File, 1989, p. 369.

7. Raymond Buckland, *Buckland's Complete Book of Witchcraft,* Llewellyn Publications, 1986, p. 5.

8. Guiley, p. 369.

9. Guiley, p. 373.

10. Guiley, p. 349.

11. Guiley, p. 350.

12. Buffalo Brownson, personal conversation.

13. From the *Mass of the Goddess,* by Diana Paxson.

STAY IN TOUCH

On the following pages you will find some of the books now available on related subjects. Your book dealer stocks most of these and will stock new titles in the Llewellyn series as they become available. We urge your patronage.

To obtain our full catalog write for our bimonthly news magazine/catalog, *Llewellyn's New Worlds of Mind and Spirit*. A sample copy is free, and it will continue coming to you at no cost as long as you are an active mail customer. Or you may subscribe for just ¢10.00 in the U.S.A. and Canada ($20.00 overseas, first class mail). Many bookstores also have *New Worlds* available to their customers. Ask for it.

Llewellyn's New Worlds of Mind and Spirit
P.O. Box 64383-567, St. Paul, MN 55164-0383, U.S.A.

TO ORDER BOOKS AND TAPES

If your book dealer does not have the books described, you may order them directly from the publisher by sending full price in U.S. funds, plus $3.00 for postage and handling for orders *under* $10.00; $4.00 for orders *over* $10.00. There are no postage and handling charges for orders over $50.00. Postage and handling rates are subject to change. We ship UPS whenever possible. Delivery guaranteed. Provide your street address as UPS does not deliver to P.O. Boxes. UPS to Canada requires a $50.00 minimum order. Allow 4-6 weeks for delivery. Orders outside the U.S.A. and Canada: Airmail—add retail price of book; add $5.00 for each non-book item (tapes, etc.); add $1.00 per item for surface mail. Mail orders to:

LLEWELLYN PUBLICATIONS
P.O. Box 64383-567, St. Paul, MN 55164-0383, U.S.A.

WHEELS OF LIFE
A User's Guide to the Chakra System
by Anodea Judith

An instruction manual for owning and operating the inner gears that run the machinery of our lives. Written in a practical, down-to-earth style, this fully illustrated book will take the reader on a journey through aspects of consciousness, from the bodily instincts of survival to the processing of deep thoughts.

Discover this ancient metaphysical system under the new light of popular Western metaphors: quantum physics, elemental magick, Kabbalah, physical exercises, poetic meditations, and visionary art. Learn how to open these centers in yourself, and see how the chakras shed light on the present world crises we face today. And learn what you can do about it!

This book will be a vital resource for: Magicians, Witches, Pagans, Mystics, Yoga Practitioners, Martial Arts people, Psychologists, Medical people, and all those who are concerned with holistic growth techniques.

The modern picture of the Chakras was introduced to the West largely in the context of Hatha and Kundalini Yoga and through the Theosophical writings of Leadbeater and Besant. But the Chakra system is equally innate to Western Magick: all psychic development, spiritual growth, and practical attainment is fully dependent upon the opening of the Chakras!

0-87542-320-5, 544 pgs., 6 x 9, illus., softcover $14.95

BUCKLAND'S COMPLETE BOOK OF WITCHCRAFT
by Raymond Buckland

Here is the most complete resource to the study and practice of modern, non-denominational Wicca. This is a lavishly illustrated, self-study course for the solitary or group. Included are rituals; exercises for developing psychic talents; information on all major "sects" of the Craft; sections on tools, beliefs, dreams, meditations, divination, herbal lore, healing, ritual clothing, and much, much more. This book unites theory and practice into a comprehensive course designed to help you develop into a practicing Witch, one of the "Wise Ones." It is written by Ray Buckland, a very famous and respected authority on Witchcraft who first came public with the Old Religion in the United States. Large format with workbook-type exercises, profusely illustrated and full of music and chants. Takes you from A to Z in the study of Witchcraft.

Never before has so much information on the Craft of the Wise been collected in one place. Traditionally, there are three degrees of advancement in most Wiccan traditions. When you have completed studying this book, you will be the equivalent of a Third-Degree Witch. Even those who have practiced Wicca for years find useful information in this book, and many covens are using this for their textbook. If you want to become a Witch, or if you merely want to find out what Witchcraft is really about, you will find no better book than this.

0-87542-050-8, 272 pgs., 8½ x 11, illus., softcover $14.95

WICCA
A Guide for the Solitary Practitioner
by Scott Cunningham

Wicca is a book of life, and how to live magically, spiritually, and wholly attuned with Nature. It is a book of sense and common sense, not only about Magick, but about religion and one of the most critical issues of today: how to achieve the much needed and wholesome relationship with our Earth. Cunningham presents Wicca as it is today: a gentle, Earth-oriented religion dedicated to the Goddess and God. This book fulfills a need for a practical guide to solitary Wicca—a need which no previous book has fulfilled.

Here is a positive, practical introduction to the religion of Wicca, designed so that any interested person can learn to practice the religion alone, anywhere in the world. It presents Wicca honestly and clearly, without the pseudo-history that permeates other books. It shows that Wicca is a vital, satisfying part of twentieth century life.

This book presents the theory and practice of Wicca from an individual's perspective. The section on the Standing Stones Book of Shadows contains solitary rituals for the Esbats and Sabbats. This book, based on the author's nearly two decades of Wiccan practice, presents an eclectic picture of various aspects of this religion. Exercises designed to develop magical proficiency, a self-dedication ritual, herb, crystal and rune magic, recipes for Sabbat feasts, are included in this excellent book.

0-87542-118-0, 240 pgs., 6 x 9, illus., softcover $9.95

LIVING WICCA
A Further Guide for the Solitary Practitioner
Scott Cunningham

Living Wicca is the long-awaited sequel to Scott Cunningham's wildly successful *Wicca: a Guide for the Solitary Practitioner*. This new book is for those who have made the conscious decision to bring their Wiccan spirituality into their everyday lives. It provides solitary practitioners with the tools and added insights that will enable them to blaze their own spiritual paths—to become their own high priests and priestesses.

Living Wicca takes a philosophical look at the questions, practices, and differences within Witchcraft. It covers the various tools of learning available to the practitioner, the importance of secrecy in one's practice, guidelines to performing ritual when ill, magical names, initiation, and the Mysteries. It discusses the benefits of daily prayer and meditation, making offerings to the gods, how to develop a prayerful attitude, and how to perform Wiccan rites when away from home or in emergency situations.

Unlike any other book on the subject, *Living Wicca* is a step-by-step guide to creating your own Wiccan tradition and personal vision of the gods, designing your personal ritual and symbols, developing your own book of shadows, and truly living your Craft.

0-87542-184-9, 208 pgs., 6 x 9, illus., softcover $10.00

WHEEL OF THE YEAR
Living the Magical Life
by Pauline Campanelli, illus. by Dan Campanelli

If you feel elated by the celebrations of the Sabbats and hunger for that feeling during the long weeks between Sabbats, *Wheel of the Year* can help you put the joy and fulfillment of magic into your everyday life. This book shows you how to celebrate the lesser changes in Nature. The wealth of seasonal rituals and charms are all easily performed with materials readily available and are simple and concise enough that the practitioner can easily adapt them to work within the framework of his or her own Pagan tradition.

Learn to perform fire magic in November, the secret Pagan symbolism of Christmas tree ornaments, the best time to visit a fairy forest or sacred spring and what to do when you get there. Learn the charms and rituals and the making of magical tools that coincide with the nesting season of migratory birds. Whether you are a newcomer to the Craft or have found your way back many years ago, *Wheel of the Year* will be an invaluable reference book in your practical magic library. It is filled with magic and ritual for everyday life and will enhance any system of Pagan Ritual.

0-87542-091-5, 176 pgs., 7 x 10, illus., softcover $9.95